First Nature Book

Photographic manipulation by Nick Wakeford and John Russell

Photo credits

p6 © Mike Wilkes/naturepl.com; p8 © Juniors Bildarchiv/Alamy; p10 © Roger Wilmshurst/Frank Lane Picture Agency/Corbis; p14 © Frank Blackburn;
Ecoscene/Corbis; p17 © Kim Taylor/Warren Photographic; p18 © Woodystock/Alamy; p20 © Photothema; p21 © Meul/Arco/naturepl.com; p22 © Kim
Taylor/naturepl.com; p24 © Kim Taylor/naturepl.com; © Fabio Cardoso/Zefa/Corbis; p26 © Julie Woodhouse/Alamy; p29 © Brian Bevan/Ardea
London Ltd; p32 © Kim Taylor/Warren Photographic; p34 © Johner Images/Getty Images; p36 © Herbert Kehier/Zefa/Corbis; p39 © Corbis;
p40 © Organics Image Library; p40 © Blickwinkel/Alamy; p42 © Ben Hall/rspb-images.com; p44 © Duncan McEwan/naturepl.com

This edition first published in 2007 by Usborne Publishing Ltd., Usborne House, 83-85 Saffron Hill, London EC1N 8RT, England. www.usborne.com
Copyright © 2007 Usborne Publishing Ltd. The name Usborne and the devices ♀ ⊕ are Trade Marks of Usborne Publishing Ltd. All rights reserved.
No part of this publication may be reproduced, stored in a retrieval system, or transmitted in any form or by any means, electronic,
mechanical, photocopying, recording or otherwise, without the prior permission of the publisher. Printed in Dubai.

First Nature Book

Illustrated by Stephen Cartwright
Written by Minna Lacey

Designed by Doriana Berkovic and Michelle Lawrence
Additional illustrations by Molly Sage

Consultants: Katrina Cook, Stuart Hine, Mandy Holloway
and Bob Press from the Natural History Museum

There is a little yellow duck to spot on every double page.

This is Apple Tree Farm.

This is Mrs. Boot the farmer. She has two children called Poppy and Sam and a dog called Rusty. Poppy and Sam love playing outside, spotting birds and butterflies and looking at flowers and trees around the farm.
You can look at nature all around you too.

Contents

Looking at birds 6

Food for the birds 8

Birds' nests 10

Insects 12

Butterflies 14

Caterpillars 16

Beetles 18

Bees 20

Grasshoppers 21

Slugs and snails 22

Earthworms 23

Creepy crawlies 24

Spiders 26

Frogs 28

Pondlife 30

Mammals 32

Flowers 34

Trees 36

Leaves 38

Fruits 40

Seeds 42

Winter buds 44

Nature diary 46

Nature words 48

Looking at birds

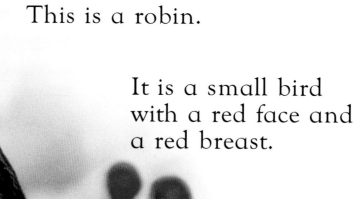

This is a robin.

It is a small bird
with a red face and
a red breast.

Robins often come
into gardens,
looking for
berries, worms
and grubs to eat.

Robins are not as shy
as other birds. If you
see one nearby, stay still;
it may come up close to you.

You may see two robins fighting, especially
in the spring. This happens if a robin lands
in an area where another robin lives.

Here are some more common
birds to look out for:

Great tit

Blue tit

Chaffinch

Song thrush

Starling

Wren

Greenfinch

Blackbird

House sparrow

When you are outside, see how
many different kinds of birds you
can spot. Listen out for their
different songs too.

od for the birds

You can attract more birds to a garden or windowsill by putting out food for them. Birds like nuts, seeds, fruit and scraps of bacon rind.

Poppy and Sam leave out food for the birds in the winter, when it is harder for birds to find food.

Bird cake

Bird cake is easy to make and full of things that birds love to eat.

These great tits are feeding on bird cake.

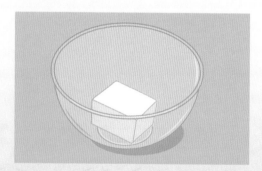

1. Put 250g (9 oz) of lard into a mixing bowl. Then, leave it until it is soft.

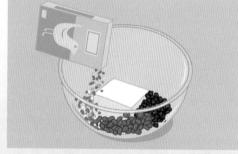

2. Add about 200g (7 oz) each of raisins, unsalted peanuts* and bird seed.

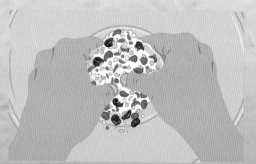

3. Mix all the ingredients together really well using your fingers.

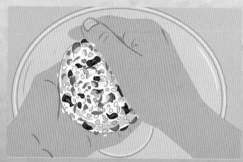

4. Shape the mixture into a rough ball, then leave it in the refrigerator to set.

Supermarkets often sell fruit in plastic nets.

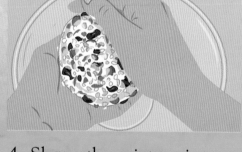

5. Put the bird cake into a plastic net and hang it up with a piece of string.

* Use unsalted peanuts because salt is not good for birds.
  If you are allergic to nuts, avoid peanuts and bird seed with nuts in.

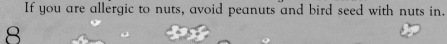

Peanuts on a string

1. Thread a large needle with string and tie a knot in the end. Push the needle through a peanut shell.

2. Push the needle through several more peanut shells. Leave enough string at the end to hang them up.

Hanging nuts

1. Fill a plastic net with unsalted peanuts. Then, tie a knot at the top.

2. Thread some string through the top of the net, like this. Then, hang it up.

9

Birds' nests

In the spring, birds build nests to lay their eggs in.

This song thrush has made a nest out of twigs, grass and moss.

Inside the nest is a smooth lining of mud.

The nest is shaped like a bowl, so the chicks don't fall out.

If you see any birds carrying twigs or grass in their beaks in spring, they are probably building a nest nearby.

Helping birds to nest

You can leave some nesting material outside to encourage birds to nest near your home.

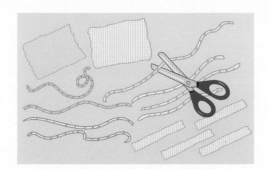

1. Cut some lengths of wool and cotton material into lots of short pieces.

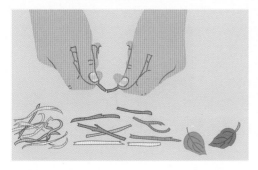

2. Collect some grasses, twigs and leaves. Break the twigs into small pieces.

3. Put all the nesting material in a pile where birds can find it easily.

Many birds use mud to make their nests. Poppy and Sam have made a small muddy patch in their garden to help birds find mud.

Insects

There are more than a million different kinds of insects in the world. Beetles and butterflies are insects, and so are grasshoppers, dragonflies and bees.

All insects have six legs.

Spiders and centipedes are not insects. They have more than six legs.

Head (top part)

Antenna for smelling and feeling

Thorax (middle part)

Eye

Claws

This is a queen wasp.

Abdomen (bottom part)

Insects' bodies are divided into three parts. Can you see them on this wasp?

Wings

Here are some common insects to spot:

Meadow brown butterfly

Green lacewing

Shield bug

Froghopper

Crane-fly (Daddy long legs)

Greenbottle fly

Magpie moth

Lots of insects come out at night and fly towards the light. You could shine a torch outside in the evening to watch how many insects fly towards it.

Butterflies

Butterflies fly around in spring and summer
feeding on nectar, a sweet juice found in flowers.

This butterfly is
called a small
tortoiseshell.

It is drinking
nectar from
a buddleia
flower.

Next time you see a butterfly land on a
flower, stay very still and look closely at it.
Can you see its long thin tongue?
It uses it like a straw to suck up nectar.

Here are some other butterflies
to look out for:

Large white

Orange tip

Common
blue

Clouded
yellow

Comma

Peacock

Red admiral

Poppy and Sam
look for butterflies
in the garden at
Apple Tree Farm.

Caterpillars

Butterflies and moths start life as caterpillars.

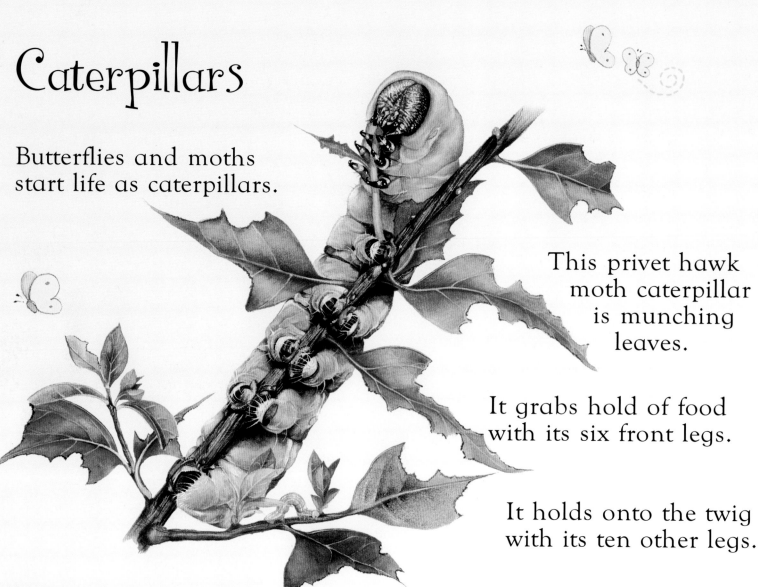

This privet hawk moth caterpillar is munching leaves.

It grabs hold of food with its six front legs.

It holds onto the twig with its ten other legs.

From a caterpillar to a butterfly or moth

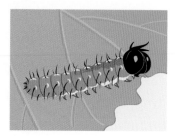

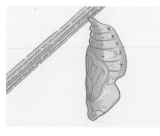

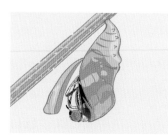

A tiny caterpillar hatches from an egg onto a leaf. It is very hungry.

It eats the leaf it hatches on. Then it eats more leaves and grows bigger.

When it is fully grown, it makes a hard case, called a pupa, around itself.

After many weeks or months, a butterfly or moth hatches out.

This painted
lady butterfly dries
its wings in the
sun, after hatching
from its pupa.

When its wings
are dry and stiff,
it will fly away.

Pupa

The best place to look for
caterpillars is on top of
and underneath leaves,
in spring and summer.

Beetles

There are lots of different kinds of beetle.
A ladybird is one kind of beetle.

Like most beetles, a ladybird has hard wing-cases.
These protect its soft wings underneath.

Wing-cases

Ladybirds
crawl over
plants, looking
for tiny greenfly
and blackfly to eat.

These yellow
ones are
ladybirds too.

Most ladybirds have spots on their back. Some
have two spots, others have seven or more. If you
see one, try to count how many spots it has.

Here are some other beetles you might see:

Nettle weevil

Stag beetle

Wasp beetle

Cardinal beetle

Bark beetle

Dung beetle

Bacon beetle

Sam and Rusty have found a beetle.

19

Bees

Bees fly from flower to flower, collecting nectar and pollen, a fine powder found inside flowers.

This is a honey bee drinking nectar from a flower. It uses the nectar to make honey.

As it drinks, pollen rubs off on its hairy body.

It stores pollen in sacs on its back legs. Pollen is used to feed young bees, called larvae.

Poppy and Sam love listening to bees buzzing in the garden in spring and summer. Bees make the noise by beating their wings very fast.

Grasshoppers

This is a common field grasshopper.

It has long powerful back legs for jumping.

A grasshopper can jump 20 times the length of its body.

Listen out for grasshoppers chirping in the long grass in fields and meadows. Then, see if you can spot one.

Slugs and snails

Slugs and snails live in damp, shady places.

Snails have a shell on their backs; slugs don't.

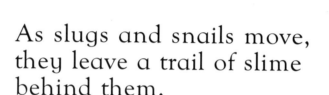

As slugs and snails move, they leave a trail of slime behind them.

The slime helps them move along and grip on to things.

Snail

Slime

Slug

Eye

Tentacles

Most slugs and snails have four tentacles on their head. The two longer ones have eyes at the end. The shorter ones are for feeling.

Earthworms

Earthworms burrow in the soil. They feed on dead plants and leaves.

This is the head end

The body is made of lots of segments.

Make a wormery

You can make your own wormery to see how earthworms tunnel in the soil.

1. Fill a plastic bottle cut in half, or a glass jar, with layers of sand and soil.

Add grass and leaves, too.

2. Dig up some earth and look for some worms. Gently place the worms in the jar.

Poke airholes in the foodwrap.

3. Tape dark paper around the sides of the jar. Cover the top with foodwrap.

4. Add a few teaspoons of water to the soil each day to keep it damp.

4. After a week, take off the paper. You'll see lots of tunnels in the soil.

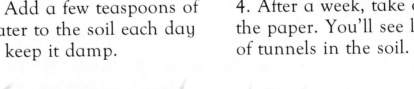

Look for earthworms at the surface of the ground after rainfall. They only come out when it's damp.

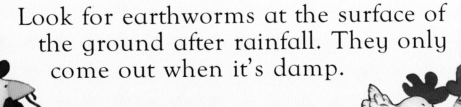

Creepy crawlies

There are lots of different kinds of creepy crawlies.

You can find them in the soil, under wood, in piles of leaves or under stones and flower pots.

Here are a few of them:

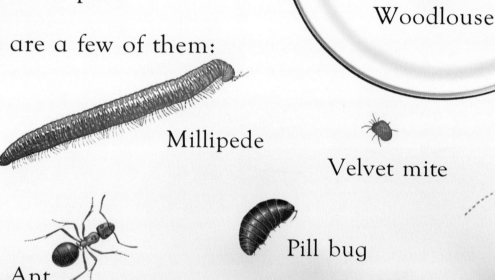

Woodlouse

Millipede

Velvet mite

Ground beetle larva

Ant

Pill bug

Earwig

This centipede has a wriggly body and moves very fast.

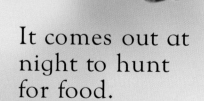

It has long antennae for feeling and smelling.

It comes out at night to hunt for food.

Collecting creepy crawlies

This is an easy way to find creepy crawlies and look at them close up.

1. Cut the top third off a plastic bottle. Place it upside down in the bottom part.

2. Fill the top part of the bottle with garden soil and dead plants and leaves.

Use a magnifying glass.

3. Leave it under a lamp for an hour. Any animals will drop into the lower part.

4. See if you can spot some creepy crawlies. Can you recognize any of them?

Poppy is looking for creepy crawlies inside a scooped out orange. If you leave half an orange upside down on the soil overnight, you may find creepy crawlies inside it the next day.

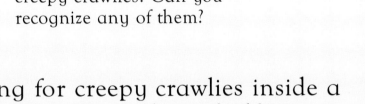

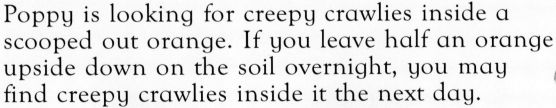

Spiders

All spiders have eight legs.
They usually have six or
eight eyes too.

Eyes

This is a
garden spider.

It makes silk
inside its body.

It uses the silk
to spin a web.

The web is a
trap for catching
insects to eat.

The silk comes
out here.

This is how a web works...

A spider senses movements
as a fly gets stuck in the web.

The spider runs quickly
across the web to the fly.

It wraps the fly in a tight
net of silk, ready for eating.

26

You can often find spiders in houses, sheds, gardens or woodpiles. Here are a few to look out for:

A house spider is large and brown with long legs.

A zebra spider is stripey and jumps on insects to catch them.

A crab spider moves sideways, like a crab.

A wolf spider is often large and hairy and runs fast.

A spitting spider spits sticky silk to trap insects.

Mrs. Boot, Sam and Rusty are looking at spiders' webs outside the window. Raindrops have collected on the webs, which makes them easier to see.

Frogs

Frogs hatch out in water, but spend much of their life hopping about on land. They belong to a group of animals called amphibians.

This is a common frog.

It catches flies and other insects with its long sticky tongue.

It has strong back legs for jumping and swimming.

Its moist skin helps it stay cool.

Its webbed toes help it to swim well.

Poppy and Sam have watched these frogs grow from frogspawn in the Apple Tree Farm pond.

How a frog grows

In the spring frogs lay their eggs in ponds, lakes or streams. The eggs are called frogspawn.

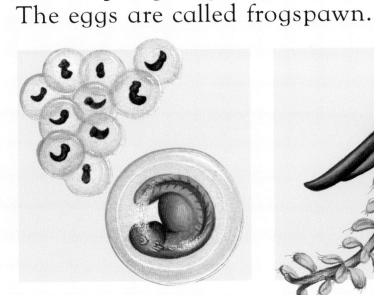

Each egg starts off looking like a tiny black dot in a blob of jelly.

After 4-5 weeks a tadpole hatches out. It wriggles its tail to swim in the water.

After 8 weeks, a tadpole grows legs. At 12-14 weeks it turns into a frog.

A common frog lays two or three thousand eggs at one time. Of these, only a few may survive and turn into adult frogs.

Pondlife

Lots of animals live
in and around ponds.

In late spring and summer,
look out for dragonflies and
damselflies above the water...

...and frogs, newts, pond-skaters
and waterboatmen in the water.

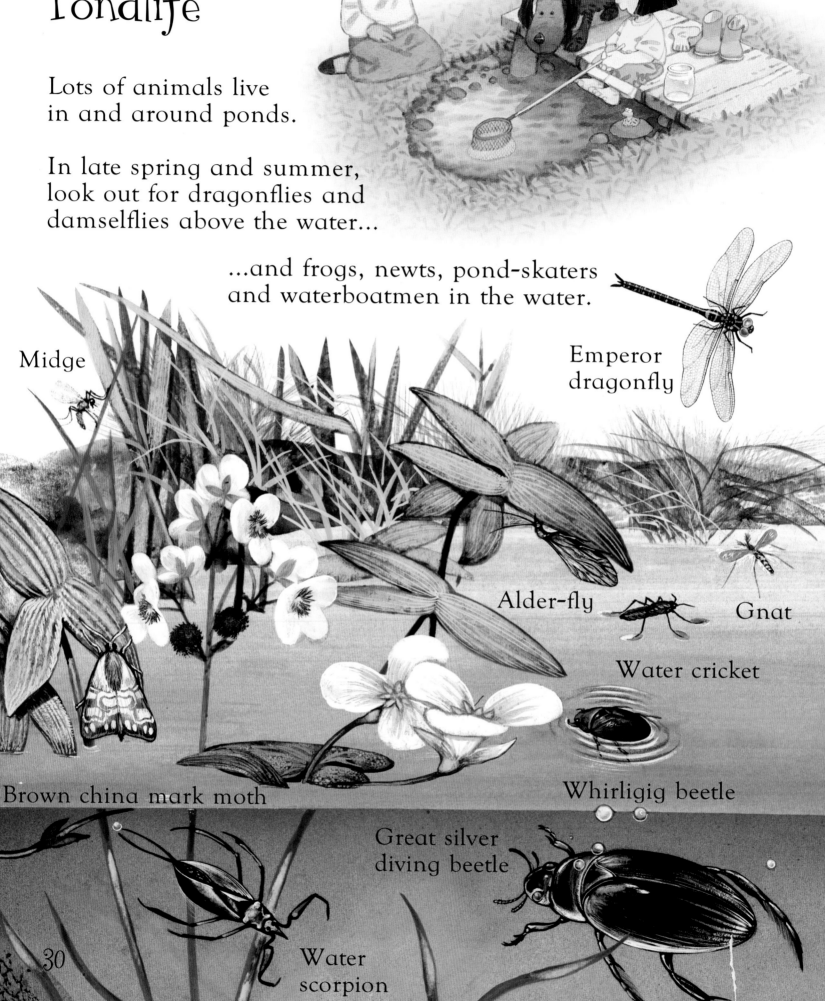

Midge

Emperor
dragonfly

Alder-fly

Gnat

Water cricket

Brown china mark moth

Whirligig beetle

Great silver
diving beetle

30

Water
scorpion

Pressing flowers

Pressed flowers make lovely decorations on cards and pictures. Make sure you check with an adult which flowers you can pick, and never pick wild flowers.

1. Pick some fresh undamaged flowers that are fully opened.

Blotting paper works best.

2. Put some thick paper in an open book. Lay the flowers on it so they are flat.

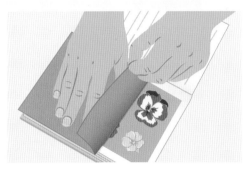

3. Lay another piece of paper on top of the flowers. Then, close the book.

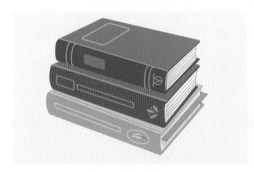

4. Stack more books on top. Leave the flowers in the book for four weeks.

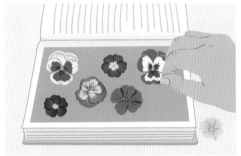

5. Carefully remove the flowers from the pages. You may need a knife to do this.

Poppy and Sam have planted sunflowers in their garden.

Trees

Trees are the largest plants in the world.

There are lots of trees on Apple Tree Farm. You can see trees everywhere; in gardens, parks, fields, woods and streets.

This is an oak tree.

Oak trees live for 300 years or more.

The outside of the tree is covered with a hard layer of bark.

Bark protects the tree from drying out, disease and from damage by animals.

Bark rubbing

Different trees have different types of bark.
You could do bark rubbings on several
different trees, to compare bark patterns.

1. Tape a piece of white
paper onto a tree trunk.

2. Rub the side of a pale
wax crayon over the paper.

3. Take the paper off the
tree and remove the tape.

4. Do some more rubbings
on different kinds of tree.

Notice the different patterns.

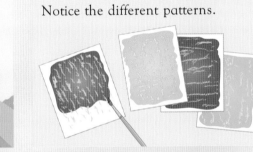

5. Paint over the rubbings
with bright watery paint.

Sam is looking at the rings
in the wood. If you count the
rings, you can find out the
age of a tree or branch.

Leaves

There are lots of different kinds of leaves.

Silver birch

Oak

Copper beech

Ash

Atlas cedar

Horse chestnut

Lime

If you look closely at a leaf you can see lines on it, called veins. Water and food travel through these.

veins

Deciduous or evergreen?

Some trees, such as oak, are deciduous. This means they lose their leaves in the autumn.

Other trees, such as holly, are evergreen. This means they keep their leaves all year.

These holly leaves have strong, waxy leaves to protect them through the cold winter months.

Leaf prints

You could collect some different leaves and use them to make leaf prints.

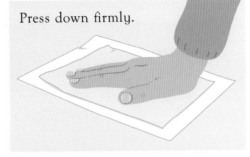

Press down firmly.

1. Paint an even layer of thick paint over the underside of a leaf.

2. Lay the leaf paintside down on some paper. Place some scrap paper on top.

3. Lift off the scrap paper. Then, carefully peel the leaf off the paper.

4. To make paler prints, print the leaf again three or four more times.

5. Collect some different leaves and make more prints in different colours.

Fruits

After a tree has flowered, it makes fruit in late summer and autumn.

Some trees make hard or prickly fruit. Others make fleshy fruit.

Acorns are the fruit of an oak tree. They have a smooth hard shell.

Acorn

Cherries are the fruit of a cherry tree. They are soft and juicy.

Cherry

Poppy and Sam are helping Mrs. Boot collect apples at the farm. Rusty wants to help, too.

Here are some more kinds
of tree fruits to look out for:

Horse chestnut

Conker

Sycamore

Apple

Beech

Blackthorn

Sloe berry

Beechnut

Pear

Douglas fir

Cone

In the autumn, you can find fruits that
have fallen to the ground. See how many
different tree fruits you can find.

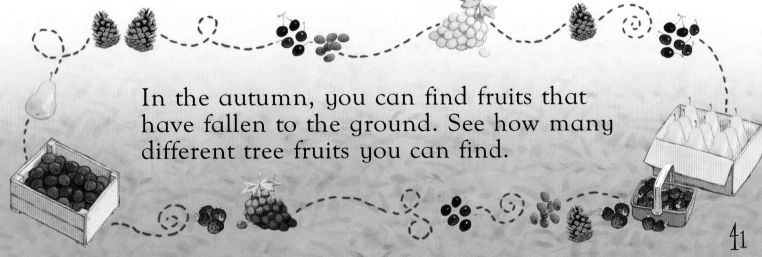

Seeds

Inside every fruit is a seed or many seeds. Each seed may grow into a new plant. When fruit ripens, the seeds are spread far and wide by birds, animals, wind or water.

This young blackbird is eating berries from a rowan tree. It eats the seeds inside the berries, too.

Later, it flies away and the seeds are spread in its droppings.

A few of the seeds may grow into new rowan trees.

Maple and sycamore seeds grow inside fruit with wings. They spin away in the wind, like helicopters.

Planting seeds

Apple pips are a type of seed. You could collect some from an apple core to grow an apple tree.

When the seedlings are big enough, move them to a bigger pot, or plant them outside.

The front of the pot has been cut away so you can see inside.

1. Put a few stones in the bottom of a plant pot. Put a saucer underneath.

2. Fill the pot with soil or seed compost. Then, water it until it is moist.

3. Use a fingertip to make a few holes in the soil, 1cm (1/2 inch) deep.

Fasten it with a rubber band.

4. Put an apple pip in each hole, then fill the holes with soil and press down firmly.

5. Put a plastic bag over the pot to keep the soil moist. Leave it in a sunny place.

It may take three weeks for a shoot to appear.

6. When a shoot appears, remove the bag. Then, water the pot twice a week.

Winter buds

In the winter, Poppy and Sam look for buds growing on twigs and branches of trees. Inside the buds are new leaves and flowers, all tightly wrapped up.

These buds are growing on a sycamore tree.

The outside of the buds are covered in tough sticky scales.

These protect the shoots inside.

Scales

The buds will open up in the spring, when it starts to grow warm.

New leaves will grow here.

If you put some twigs with winter buds in a vase of water, you can force the buds to open early.

Here are some twigs and winter buds to look out for:

Walnut

Magnolia

Sweet chestnut

Beech

Wild cherry

Willow

45

Nature diary

Spring

In the spring, the weather grows warmer and trees burst into leaf. Birds start to build nests and on the farm, many animals give birth to their young.

Look out for fruit trees sprinkled with blossom and early spring flowers peeping out of the ground.

Summer

In the summer, it is sunny and warm and trees are covered in green leaves. Poppy and Sam like looking for wild flowers in meadows and hedgerows at the farm.

Look out for birds feeding their fluffy young chicks and lots of insects flying, such as butterflies, bees and dragonflies.

Autumn

In the autumn, the weather grows colder and many leaves turn orange and fall to the ground.

Look out for mushrooms growing in woods and fields, big garden spiders and squirrels burying nuts.

Poppy and Sam like to play with the leaves and look for fallen fruits and seeds, such as acorns and conkers.

Winter

In the winter, the weather turns cold and the ground looks bare.

Many animals, including mice, hedgehogs, frogs, bats and snakes, go into a deep sleep called hibernation.

Poppy and Sam love making a snowman when it snows and looking for ice in ponds and puddles.

47

Nature words

abdomen
The bottom part of an insect's body.

amphibian
An animal that hatches out in water, but lives on land and in water, such as a frog, toad or newt.

antenna (plural: antennae)
Long feelers on the head of insects and other creepy crawlies, used for sensing things.

beetle
A type of insect with hard wing-cases, or front wings, on its back.

compost
A rich soily mixture for growing plants in.

deciduous
A deciduous tree loses its leaves in autumn and winter.

evergreen
An evergreen tree keeps its leaves all year round.

grub
A young insect or larva.

hibernate
To spend the winter months in a deep, long sleep.

insect
A small animal with three body parts, six legs and often two pairs of wings.

larva (plural: larvae)
A young insect, before it starts changing into its adult form.

mammal
A warm-blooded animal with hair on its body. Female mammals make milk in their body to feed their young.

nectar
A sugary liquid found in flowers.

pollen
A fine powder found inside flowers.

pupa
An insect at a stage between changing from a larva into an adult.

thorax
The middle part of an insect's body.

veins
The lines on leaves, through which food and water travel.

Table of Contents

Beware the Full Moon!. 4

What Is a Werewolf?. 6

Becoming a Werewolf. 8

How to Spot a Werewolf. 10

Killing a Werewolf. 12

Early Werewolves 14

The Great Werewolf Hunts. 16

The Beast of Gévaudan 18

Other Were-Creatures. 20

The World of Shape-Shifters. 22

Werewolves in Books 24

Werewolves in Movies 26

Warriors and Wolves. 28

Fact or Fiction? 30

Glossary and Index. 32

Beware the Full Moon!

A full moon lights up the sky. A loud howl fills the air, striking fear into the bravest heart. Watch out! A werewolf is on the hunt for human flesh!

Most of us only know about werewolves from movies and television. Some people, however, say that werewolves are real. A few even claim to have been attacked by these terrifying monsters.

Do such creatures really exist? According to the **legends** and **lore** presented in this book, they do. These stories have been told at many different times and in many different places. Read on and decide for yourself if werewolves actually roam the planet.

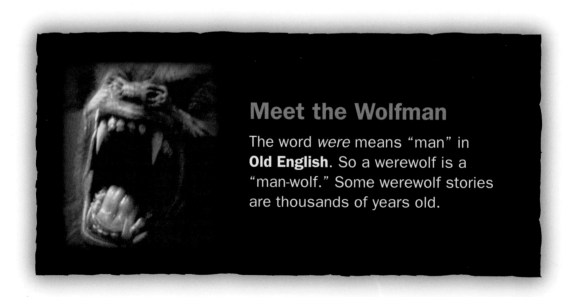

Meet the Wolfman

The word *were* means "man" in **Old English**. So a werewolf is a "man-wolf." Some werewolf stories are thousands of years old.

What Is a Werewolf?

What do most people think of when they picture a werewolf? Most likely, they see a person who turns into a wolf when the moon is full. By night, the werewolf is a **savage** killer, attacking anyone it meets. By day, it is human again.

Not all werewolves look and act the same, however, according to the stories that have been handed down. For example, in early Native American legends, wolfmen walked on all fours. In later legends, they began to walk on two legs. In some European legends, werewolves can talk while they are wolves. In other stories, they are just howling beasts.

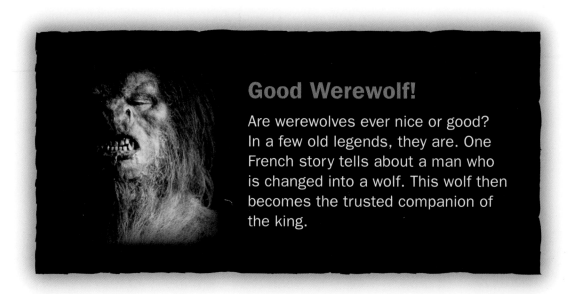

Good Werewolf!

Are werewolves ever nice or good? In a few old legends, they are. One French story tells about a man who is changed into a wolf. This wolf then becomes the trusted companion of the king.

Becoming a Werewolf

In stories and movies, people usually become werewolves because they are under a **curse**. The curse might be the work of a **sorcerer**. It might also begin with a bite from a werewolf. Other causes are drinking water from a wolf's paw-print or swimming in a cursed stream.

Most people cursed with being werewolves don't like it. They feel terrible about killing others, but they can't help themselves. Some werewolves try to get themselves killed in order to be rid of the curse. A few, however, do enjoy having the superhuman strength and speed of a werewolf.

Wolf Magic

German werewolves are called boxenwolves. People change into these creatures by putting magic straps around their bodies. Horses are boxenwolves' favorite food. In one German village, a man knew how to whisper magic words into the ears of horses. The words protected the horses against the boxenwolves.

How to Spot a Werewolf

People change into werewolves when there is a full moon. The rest of the time, they look and behave like everyone else—except for a few unusual **traits**.

Some of the best-known legends say that there are certain clues that help show that a person is a werewolf. The three main signs are rough hair on the palms, an extra-long index finger, and extremely thick eyebrows that meet in the middle.

A werewolf's habits can also give the creature away. Many werewolves avoid running water, such as rivers and streams. Werewolves also hate light. In some legends they can't even look up at the daytime sky.

Tell-Tale Smells

Some legends say that a person can sniff out a werewolf. Werewolves are believed to have very bad breath and terrible body odor!

Killing a Werewolf

In old movies, only a silver bullet can kill a werewolf. This idea can be traced back to real events in Europe. In the 1600s and 1700s, people who were thought to be werewolves were killed with bullets made from silver objects that had been melted down.

In many werewolf stories, however, any weapon that kills a normal wolf will kill a werewolf. Shotguns, spears, traps, and poison have all been used.

What should a person do once the creature is dead? The stories say one must cut off its head, burn the body, and then scatter the ashes. Now the werewolf's curse is broken. Anyone once bitten by this werewolf becomes human again.

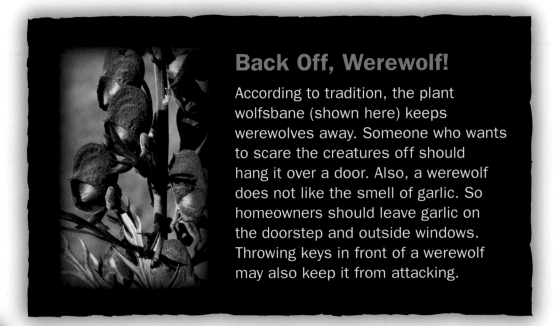

Back Off, Werewolf!

According to tradition, the plant wolfsbane (shown here) keeps werewolves away. Someone who wants to scare the creatures off should hang it over a door. Also, a werewolf does not like the smell of garlic. So homeowners should leave garlic on the doorstep and outside windows. Throwing keys in front of a werewolf may also keep it from attacking.

Early Werewolves

Werewolves are as old as storytelling. The *Epic of Gilgamesh*, written 4,000 years ago, features a werewolf-like man named Enkidu. At first he roams the **steppes** of ancient Babylonia (*bab*-ih-LOH-nee-uh) with wild animals. Later, he goes off to live among humans.

Members of a secret religion in ancient Greece believed that jumping into a lake would change them into wolves. In 400 BC, a member of this group, Damarchus, won a boxing match at the ancient Greek Olympics. It is said he changed into a wolf during the fight.

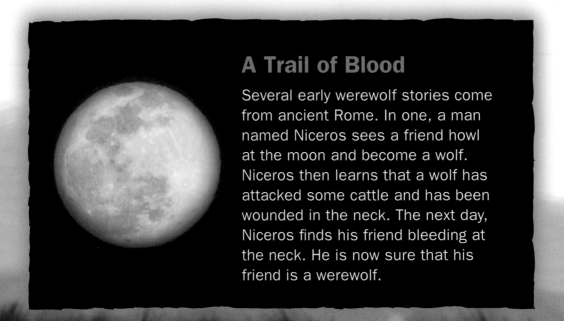

A Trail of Blood

Several early werewolf stories come from ancient Rome. In one, a man named Niceros sees a friend howl at the moon and become a wolf. Niceros then learns that a wolf has attacked some cattle and has been wounded in the neck. The next day, Niceros finds his friend bleeding at the neck. He is now sure that his friend is a werewolf.

The Great Werewolf Hunts

During the **Middle Ages** in Europe, people took werewolves very seriously. Many saw them as evil killers. The citizens of Vicenza, Italy, decided on a way to protect themselves. In 1300, they built high walls to keep werewolves out of their town!

The widespread fear also led to werewolf hunts and trials. In Germany and Serbia, people who were found guilty of being werewolves had their heads cut off and their bodies burned.

From 1520 to 1630, thousands of people across Europe were killed for being werewolves. They were accused of stealing cattle and killing children. Many people admitted to being werewolves after they were horribly tortured.

Belts, Buckles, and Bullets

In the year 1640, in the town of Greifswald, Germany, many people were dying. It was thought that werewolves were responsible. A group of students decided to take action. They melted down silver buckles and belts to make silver bullets. With these bullets, the students hunted and shot the so-called werewolves.

The Beast of Gévaudan

One of the most famous werewolf-like creatures in history is known as the "Beast of Gévaudan" (ZHAY-voh-dahn). Between 1764 and 1767, the Beast is said to have killed about 100 people in the mountains of south-central France. Whole villages were deserted as people fled in terror.

King Louis XV sent France's best hunters to stop the Beast. In 1765, they were sure they had killed it. However, attacks on people began again a few months later. Finally, a local hunter killed a large wolf-like animal, and the attacks ended. Some say he used a gun loaded with silver bullets.

What Really Happened?

Many of the attacks and deaths blamed on the Beast of Gévaudan really occurred. No one has ever been able to explain what caused them, however. Some people still claim that the Beast was a werewolf. Other **theories** say that it was a person posing as a werewolf, or it was a lion that had escaped from a zoo.

Other Were-Creatures

Stories of werewolves are common in parts of the world where wolves have lived. Other were-creatures—humans that turn into animals—also appear in stories from many cultures.

In Russia, people become were-bears, and in Peru, they turn into were-jaguars. In Chile, there are witches who turn into creatures that are a mix of vulture, lion, and human. In Indian folklore, people change into were-tigers and were-foxes.

Were-foxes are also very popular in the legends of China and Japan. Unlike werewolves, they do not start out as humans. In China, it was believed that a fox who lived 500 years could change into a human!

Tricky Tales

The Japanese were-fox, called a *kitune*, is usually female. Its bushy tail can be seen even when it is in human form. A kitune turns back into a fox at night and plays tricks on people.

The World of Shape-Shifters

A shape-shifter is a person who can change form—usually becoming an animal. Werewolves are one kind of shape-shifter. There are many other kinds in **myths** and legends from around the world.

The Navajo (NAV-uh-*hoh*) people of the southwestern United States tell stories about "skin-walkers." A skin-walker is a healer who uses **supernatural** powers to change into an animal such as a wolf, bear, or eagle.

In Mexican folklore, the *nahual* are witches who turn into wolves, jaguars, or eagles before attacking an enemy. In Iceland, a *hamrammr* is a were-creature that changes into the animal it has just eaten. Its strength increases with each animal it gobbles up.

Fast-Running Skin-Walkers

According to tradition, a skin-walker becomes a wolf in order to travel great distances quickly. In 1970, four young men were traveling to the town of Zuni in New Mexico. They reported seeing a two-legged skin-walker running alongside their car. They were driving at 60 mph (97 kph)!

Werewolves in Books

Werewolf stories have been around for thousands of years. For a long time, however, they were told mostly by word of mouth. Books about werewolves became popular only in the 1800s.

Wagner the Wehr-Wolf was written by G. W. M. Reynolds in the 1840s. Its main character makes a deal with the devil. He can live forever but has to become a werewolf every seven years.

Robert Louis Stevenson's *The Strange Case of Dr. Jekyll and Mr. Hyde* was published in 1886. In it, a scientist creates a drug that turns him into a murdering, werewolf-like beast.

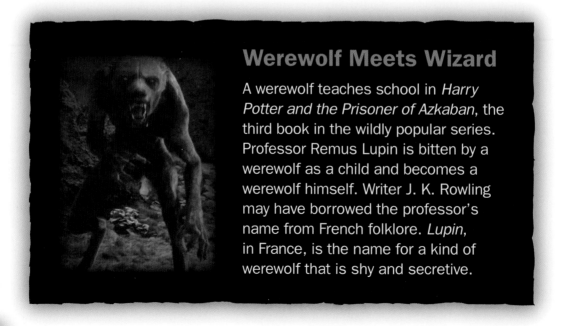

Werewolf Meets Wizard

A werewolf teaches school in *Harry Potter and the Prisoner of Azkaban*, the third book in the wildly popular series. Professor Remus Lupin is bitten by a werewolf as a child and becomes a werewolf himself. Writer J. K. Rowling may have borrowed the professor's name from French folklore. *Lupin*, in France, is the name for a kind of werewolf that is shy and secretive.

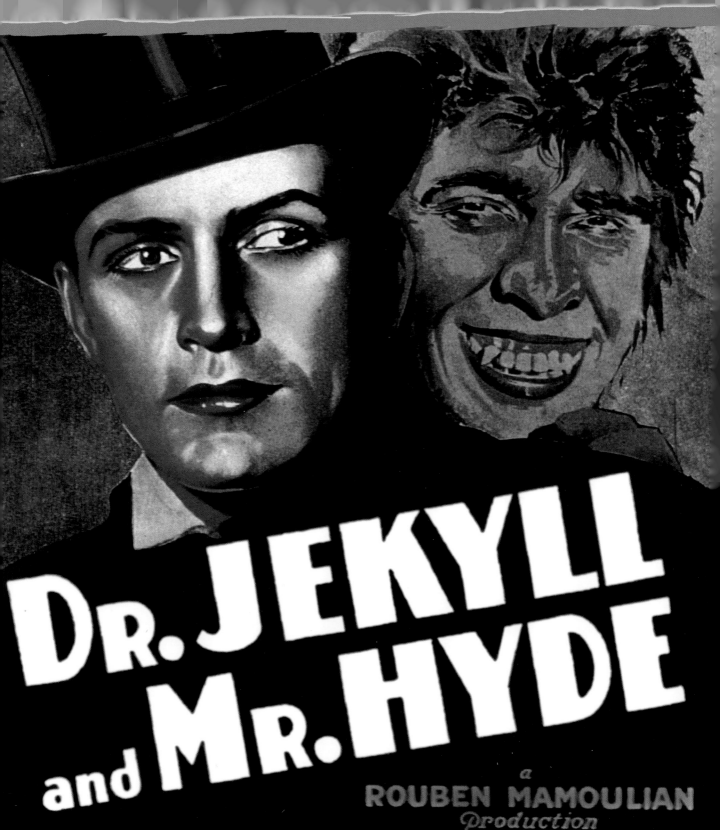

DR. JEKYLL and MR. HYDE

a
ROUBEN MAMOULIAN
Production

WITH
FREDRIC MARCH

25

Werewolves in Movies

Movies became a popular form of entertainment in the early 1900s. Since that time, werewolves have been a favorite movie subject.

In 1913, the silent film *The Werewolf* used a real wolf in the title role. Later films, such as *The Werewolf of London* (1935) and *The Wolfman* (1941), used actors with hairy makeup. In recent films, such as *Van Helsing* (2004), the werewolves are created by computer graphics.

One of the newest werewolf-like movie characters, Wolverine, started out on the printed page. In the *X-Men* comic books and movies (2000, 2003, 2006), Wolverine is a wolf-like superhero with sharp **talons** on the ends of his fingers.

Creature Features

There have been many movies starring were-creatures other than werewolves. In *Cat People* (1942), a beautiful woman turns into a black panther. In *The Fly* (1958), a scientist turns into a giant fly after an experiment goes terribly wrong.

WEREWOLF OF LO

HENRY HULL VALERIE HOB

Warriors and Wolves

Where do werewolf stories come from? Some people say that they may have come from true stories about fierce **warriors**.

Hundreds of years ago, many warriors wore animal skins because they believed the **garments** would turn them into good fighters. Wearing skins also made them look like scary monsters!

In medieval Germany, people also believed that great warriors became wolves when they died. Boys were called Wolfbrand and Wolfgang to make them strong and brave.

Viking warriors called berserkers wore bearskin shirts. They howled like animals when they charged their enemies. No wonder people thought they were being attacked by were-bears!

The Leopard Men

The Leopard Men were a secret group of warriors in West Africa. A Leopard Man wore the skin of a leopard and an iron bracelet that had dangling knives. When he clenched his fist, the knives became claws. Local chiefs paid members of the Leopard Men to kill enemies.

Fact or Fiction?

Almost everyone agrees that werewolves are not real. Yet many people in the past believed they were. Why?

Some people may have looked or acted like werewolves because of physical or mental illness. For example, more than 2,000 years ago, King Nebuchadnezzar (*neb*-uh-kuhd-NEZ-uhr) of ancient Babylonia went mad. He thought he was a wolf and let his hair grow wild.

Many people in Europe admitted to being werewolves—but only after being tortured. Some people were quick to call others "werewolves." After all, they didn't want to be accused themselves!

Rare Diseases?

Some people thought to be werewolves may have had a condition known as hypertrichosis (*hye*-per-trih-KOH-sis). This illness makes a person incredibly hairy.

Another rare disease, porphyria (por-FIHR-ee-uh), also makes people look like werewolves. Their skin changes color, thick hair grows on their face, and they become sensitive to light.

Even if werewolves are not real, however, stories about them are still popular. So in a way these creatures do exist—if only in people's minds and imaginations.

Glossary

curse (KURSS) something that causes evil or injury; a spell

garments (GAR-muhnts) pieces of clothing

legends (LEJ-uhnds) stories that are handed down from the past and are generally believed to be true by those who tell them

lore (LOR) a collection of traditional stories

Middle Ages (MID-uhl AJE-iz) a time period in European history from about AD 500 to around 1500

myths (MITHS) traditional stories that often tell of larger-than-life beings and mysterious events

Old English (OHLD ING-glish) the early form of English that was spoken until about AD 1100

savage (SAV-ij) wild and fierce

sorcerer (SOR-sur-er) someone, such as a witch or wizard, who performs magic

steppes (STEPS) grasslands in parts of Europe and Asia

supernatural (soo-pur-NACH-ur-*uhl*) something unusual that breaks the laws of nature

talons (TAL-uhnz) claws

theories (THIHR-eez) ideas that explain certain facts or events

traits (TRATES) characteristics

Viking (VYE-king) a member of a group of warriors who lived from the late 700s to about 1100 in the area that is now Norway, Sweden, and Denmark

warriors (WOR-ee-urz) fighters

Index

ancient Greece 14
ancient Rome 14
Beast of Gévaudan 18–19
berserkers 28
books 24
boxenwolves 8
Cat People 26
Chile 20
China 20
Epic of Gilgamesh 14
European legends 6
The Fly 26
France 6, 18, 24
Germany 8, 16, 28
hamrammr 22

Iceland 22
Indian folklore 20
Japan 20
King Louis XV 18
King Nebuchadnezzar 30
kitune 20
Leopard Men 28
Mexican folklore 22
Middle Ages 16
movies 4, 8, 12, 26
nahual 22
Native American legends 6
Navajo people 22
Old English 4

Olympics 14
Peru 20
Reynolds, G. W. M. 24
Rowling, J. K. 24
Russia 20
Serbia 16
shape-shifters 22
silver bullets 12, 16, 18
skin-walkers 22
Stevenson, Robert Louis 24
The Strange Case of Dr. Jekyll and Mr. Hyde 24
television 4
trials 16
Van Helsing 26

Vicenza, Italy 16
Vikings 28
Wagner the Wehr-Wolf 24
were-bears 20, 28
were-creatures 20, 22
were-foxes 20
were-jaguars 20
were-tigers 20
The Werewolf 26
The Werewolf of London 26
The Wolfman 26
wolfsbane 12
Wolverine 26
X-Men 26